My First Riddle

London & The South Of England

Edited by Connie Hunt

First published in Great Britain in 2011 by:

Young Writers

Remus House
Coltsfoot Drive
Peterborough
PE2 9BF
Telephone: 01733 890066
Website: www.youngwriters.co.uk

Foreword

'My First Riddle' was a competition specifically designed for Key Stage 1 children. The simple, fun form of the riddle gives even the youngest and least confident writers the chance to become interested in poetry by giving them a framework within which to shape their ideas. As well as this it also allows older children to let their creativity flow as much as possible, encouraging the use of simile and descriptive language.

Given the young age of the entrants, we have tried to include as many poems as possible. We believe that seeing their work in print will inspire a love of reading and writing and give these young poets the confidence to develop their skills in the future.

Our defining aim at Young Writers is to foster the talent of the next generation of authors. We are proud to present this latest collection of anthologies and hope you agree that they are an excellent showcase of young writing talent.

Contents

Wrestlingworth Lower School, Wrestlingworth

The Poems

My Grandma

She is as kind as a horse
She is as lovely as a princess
She is my grandma, Pat.

Sophia Bellau (5)
Annemount School, Hampstead

My Grandfather

He is as kind as a mother
He is very sporty
He likes having fun
He cooks like a chef
He is a sailor
He is my grandfather.

Dexter James (6)
Annemount School, Hampstead

My Mummy

She's as clever as a scientist.
She's as funny as a comedian.
She's as lovely as a butterfly.
She's as cross as a tiger.
She's as happy as the sunshine.

Leo Calman-Finlay (7)
Annemount School, Hampstead

Annabella

She's as lovely as autumn leaves.
She's as creative as a picture.
She's as playful as a dog.
She's as neat as the classroom.
She's as bright as the light.

Nathan Simon (6)
Annemount School, Hampstead

My Sister

She's as sweet as a star.
She's as funny as a clown.
She's as sleepy as a bee.
She's as good as a museum.

Natalia Toffel (6)
Annemount School, Hampstead

Guess Who? Me!

She's as funny as a clown.
She's as happy as a party.
She's s nice as a good friend.
She's as arty as an art teacher.
She's as big as a giant.

Jessica Levine (6)
Annemount School, Hampstead

My Mummy

She is as lovely as a princess
She is as kind as a mum
She is as beautiful as the moon
She is as strict as a dragon
She is my mummy.

Jordan Marsh (5)
Annemount School, Hampstead

My Brother

I love him
He is as cute as a bunny
He is as cuddly as a berry
He is my brother.

Tara Nikoopour (5)
Annemount School, Hampstead

My Grandma

She is as clever as a scientist
She is as good at boxing as a boxer
She is as strict as a dragon
She is as lovely as a star
She cooks as well as a TV chef
She is my grandma.

Anna Rutland (6)
Annemount School, Hampstead

My Sister

She loves her friends
She is more beautiful than the sun
She is as funny as a clown
She is as pretty as a princess
She is as nice as a teenager
She is my sister, Anouska.

Mannie Reeback (5)
Annemount School, Hampstead

My Mum

She is as kind as a princess.
She is as good a cook as a chef.
She cuddles me as a bear.
She is my mum.

Arav Raja (6)
Annemount School, Hampstead

My Nanny-Ma

She is as sweet as chocolate
She is as kind as a good fairy
She cooks yummy dhal and rice
She is my nannyma.

Lillian Rodney (6)
Annemount School, Hampstead

My Dad

He is as strong as a giant.
He is as good at catching as a bird.
He is my dad.

Yaroslav Chalou (5)
Annemount School, Hampstead

My Brother

He is as crazy as a car
He likes football
He likes Ben 10
He is my brother, Sam.

Tamara Callman (5)
Annemount School, Hampstead

My Mum

She is better than a TV chef.
She is stricter than a dragon.
She is as nice as a horse.
She is my mum.

Elizabeth Dean (5)
Annemount School, Hampstead

My Dad

He is as strict as a dragon
He is as nice as a horse
He is as funny as a monkey
He is as fast as a rhino
He is as big as a tiger
He is my dad.

Luke Johnson (5)
Annemount School, Hampstead

My Cousin

She is as young as a baby
She is as clever as a musician
She is as gentle as a feather
She is as lovely as cake
She is my cousin, Kate.

Amy Solomon (5)
Annemount School, Hampstead

My Cousin

He is as nice as a horse
He is as funny as a clown
He likes to make things
He glows like the moon
He is my cousin, Anish.

Raghav Kanwar (5)
Annemount School, Hampstead

My Grandma

She makes necklaces
She is as kind as a butterfly
She is as sweet as honey
She is my grandma.

Isabella Gardiner (5)
Annemount School, Hampstead

My Cousin

He is as funny as a clown
He is on Blue Peter
He is as nice as apple pie
He has a Nintendo DS
He is Joshua, my cousin.

Priya Rodney (6)
Annemount School, Hampstead

My Grandma

She is a very good pasta cook
She's as old as a dinosaur
She has a freedom pass
She's as free as a bird
She likes looking at me and forgets where she puts things
She is my grandma.

Eliyahu Gluschove-Koppel (5)
Annemount School, Hampstead

My Brother

He is as cuddly as a teddy bear
He is as cute as a rabbit
He is as chubby as a squashed banana
He is my brother, Alon.

Maia Jaffe (6)
Annemount School, Hampstead

Untitled

She is as beautiful as a flower.
She is as kind as a mummy.
She is as good as a daddy.
She is as charming as a prince.
She is as sweet as a diamond.
She is Cinderella.

Ottilie Swan (6)
Bloxham CE Primary School, Bloxham

Untitled

He is as fast as a cheetah.
He is as cool as a game.
He knows more skills than ever.
He is as sweaty as a goose.
He is as tough as a bear.
He is Steven Gerrard.

Robert Pollard (6)
Bloxham CE Primary School, Bloxham

Untitled

He is as mean as a tiger.
He is as ugly as a fox.
He is as fierce as a lion.
He is as stupid as a bear.
He is as noisy as a leopard.
He is a T-rex.

Ruby Lapper (6)
Bloxham CE Primary School, Bloxham

What Is It?

It is as fast as a bird
It is as nasty as a bat
It is as quick as a football
It is as creepy as a beetle
It is as fierce as a wolf
It is a spider.

Oliver Hall (6)
Bloxham CE Primary School, Bloxham

Untitled

Michael Jackson is
As intelligent as a doctor
As amazing as a disco dancer
As fantastic as a super singer.

**Martha Howard, Priya Kommu, Kurt, Ophelia Swan, Connor Butler & Emma
Street (5)**
Bloxham CE Primary School, Bloxham

She Is

She is as kind as a little girl
She is a big girl
She has mice friends and bird friends
She is a housemaid
She has the voice of an angel
She has been to the ball
She is elegant and graceful
She is Cinderella.

Charlotte Cartwright (6)
Bloxham CE Primary School, Bloxham

Guess Which Princess!

She is as kind as a kitten.
She is as pretty as a deer.
She is as helpful as Prince Charming.
She is as caring as a cat.
She moves like a nightingale.
She dances like an angel.
She looks like a famous dancer.
She sings like a bird.
She is Cinderella.

Sophie Jackson (6)
Bloxham CE Primary School, Bloxham

Untitled

It is as fast as a monster.
It is as horrible as a person.
It is as black as the night.
It is as fast as a car.
It is as hairy as my dad's legs.
It is as dangerous as a boat.
You will not want to hold it.
It is a spider!

Hannah Maycock (6)
Bloxham CE Primary School, Bloxham

He Is . . .

He is as fast as a cheetah.
He is as quick as a shooting star.
He is as quick as a man with his pants on fire.
He is Steven Gerrard.

Lottie Rice (7)
Bloxham CE Primary School, Bloxham

Untitled

It is as pretty as the stars in the sky.
It is as kind as an angel.
It is as colourful as a book.
It is as beautiful as an apple.
It is as lovely as a rainbow.
It is as helpful as the abc.
It is a butterfly.

Saskia Kaura (6)
Bloxham CE Primary School, Bloxham

Untitled

She is as kind as a sweet butterfly.
She is as slow as a giraffe.
She is really, really nicely dressed as a queen.
She is Cinderella.

Maddy England (6)
Bloxham CE Primary School, Bloxham

Untitled

A dinosaur is as fierce as a lion.
A dinosaur is as mean as a tiger.
A dinosaur is as ugly as a skeleton.
A dinosaur is as stupid as a frog.
A dinosaur is as noisy as a jack-in-the-box.
A dinosaur is as nasty as a crow.
He is a T-rex.

Lauren Humphreys (6)
Bloxham CE Primary School, Bloxham

Untitled

She is as sweet as cake.
She is as cuddly as a koala.
She is as cute as a puppy.
She is as funny as my dad.
She is as bonkers as a man with his pants on fire.
She is my cat, Poppy.

Daisy Beck (6) & Amber
Bloxham CE Primary School, Bloxham

She's As . . .

She's as cute as a kiwi.
She's as cuddly as a cub.
She's as soft as a polar bear.
She's as fast as a cheetah.
She's as stripy as a zebra.
She's a cat.

Isobel Cox (6)
Bloxham CE Primary School, Bloxham

Untitled

He's as cool as David Beckham.
He's as fast as a cheetah.
He's as kind as my brother.
He's as skilful as Fabregas.
He's as tall as a giraffe.
He's as crazy as a monkey.
He's as sweaty as a sauna.
He's Steven Gerrard.

Hamish Nelson (6)
Bloxham CE Primary School, Bloxham

Untitled

A dinosaur is as strong as Batman,
A dinosaur is as tough as bricks.
A dinosaur is as gigantic as London.

Oliver Hughes (6)
Bloxham CE Primary School, Bloxham

Untitled

He is as fast as a cheetah.
He is as cool as a game.
He is as loud as a lion.
He is as famous as a new game.
He is as good as my mum.
He has more skills than ever.
He is Steven Gerrard.

Amber-Rose Troops (6)
Bloxham CE Primary School, Bloxham

SpongeBob

He is as funny as a clown.
He is as silly as a joker.
He is as straight as a man with his pants folded down.

Thomas Foster (6)
Bloxham CE Primary School, Bloxham

Untitled

He is as fast as a cheetah.
He is as famous as the sun.
He is as good as an angel.
He is as strong as a dog.
He is as cool as my daddy.
He is as kind as Mollie.
He is as nice as my mummy.
He is as quick as my cat.
He is Steven Gerrard.

Abbi Lester (6)
Bloxham CE Primary School, Bloxham

Untitled

He is as fast as a shooting star.
He is as cool as my daddy.
He is nicer than a flower.
He is as skilful as a frog.
He is as cuddly as a cat.
He is as sweaty as a goose.
He is Steven Gerrard.

Mollie Lester (6)
Bloxham CE Primary School, Bloxham

My Riddle

She is as kind as a puppy.
She is as brave as a lion.
She is as lovely as flowers.
She is as naughty as my sister.
She is as graceful as a butterfly.
She is as beautiful as chocolate.
Who is it?
She is my mum.

liesha Rickard (6)
Bloxham CE Primary School, Bloxham

My Riddle

He is as brave as a bull.
He is as funny as a clown.
He is as cuddly as a teddy.
He is as clever as a fox.
He is as fast as a cheetah.
He is as brainy as a wizard.
Who is it?
My dad.

William Byrd (7)
Bloxham CE Primary School, Bloxham

My Riddle

He is as fast as a cheetah.
He is as kind as a mum.
He is as friendly as a girl.
He is as good as an angel.
He is as happy as a king.
He is as funny as a joker.
Who is it?
Jay.

Oscar Byrne (6)
Bloxham CE Primary School, Bloxham

Untitled

She is as cheeky as a monkey
She is as naughty as a fish
She is as sweet as a puppy
She is as cuddly as a teddy
It is my sister, Talia.

Elana Lloyd-Edwards
Brambletye Preparatory School, East Grinstead

Untitled

She is as spotty as a ladybird
She is as fast as a tiger
She is as licky as a leopard
She is as sniffy as a cheetah
She is as waggy as a cow
She is Holly, my dog.

Robert Adams (5)
Brambletye Preparatory School, East Grinstead

Untitled

She is as pretty as a bird
She is as happy as a hyena
She is as lovely as a horse
She is as friendly as a fish
She is a cowgirl.

Maja Marten
Brambletye Preparatory School, East Grinstead

Untitled

It is as slippery as slime
It is as thin as a stick
It is as long as a hosepipe
It is as smooth as glass
It is as quick as a flash
It is a snake.

Lois Russell
Brambletye Preparatory School, East Grinstead

Untitled

She is as cuddly as a teddy bear
She is as small as a puppy
She is as fluffy as a rabbit
She is as cute as a baby
She is Tinker, my cat.

Alice Butt
Brambletye Preparatory School, East Grinstead

Untitled

It is as slippery as slime
It is as thin as a stick
It is as long as a hosepipe
It is as smooth as glass
It is as quick as a flash
It is a snake.

Phoebe Wiseman (6)
Brambletye Preparatory School, East Grinstead

Untitled

He is as fast as a mouse
He is as cheeky as a monkey
He is as cute as a puppy
He is as naughty as a bear
He is Boris, my dog.

Topsy Holder
Brambletye Preparatory School, East Grinstead

Untitled

It is as strong as a bear
It is as magical as a unicorn
It is as precious as a mummy
It is as good as a present
It is my dragon.

Eddy Heffernan (5)
Brambletye Preparatory School, East Grinstead

Untitled

It is as slippery as slime
It is as thin as a stick
It is as smooth as glass
It is as long as a hosepipe
It is as smooth as glass
It is as quick as a flash
It is a snake.

Annabelle Orgill
Brambletye Preparatory School, East Grinstead

Untitled

She is as pretty as sparkly shoes
She is as friendly as a princess
She is as smiley as a teacher
She is as pretty as a flower
She is Lizzy.

Lexi Hudson (4)
Brambletye Preparatory School, East Grinstead

Untitled

She is as pretty as a butterfly
She is as beautiful as a queen
She is as friendly as a fairy
She is as kind as my friends
It is Lisa, my mummy.

Hermione Gearon (5)
Brambletye Preparatory School, East Grinstead

Untitled

He is as brave as a soldier.
He is as famous as a pop star.
He is as amazing as a bat.
He is as skilled as James Bond.
He is as black as night.
He is Batman.

Thomas Wilson (6)
Brambletye Preparatory School, East Grinstead

Untitled

He is as awesome as an army jet.
He is as funny as a clown.
He dances as coolly as the moonwalk.
He is as famous as a movie star.
He is as popular as the Statue of Liberty.
His hair is as long as spaghetti.
He is Michael Jackson.

Alexandra Adam (6)
Brambletye Preparatory School, East Grinstead

Untitled

He is as cuddly as a teddy bear.
He is as much fun as swimming.
He is as soft as sugar.
He is as fluffy as a sheep.
He is as playful as a baby lamb.
He sleeps as quietly as a mouse.
He is as gold as runny honey.
He is Leo, my dog.

Sophie Miller (6)
Brambletye Preparatory School, East Grinstead

Untitled

He is as wiggly as a snake
His fins are as flappy as birds' wings
He swims as fast as a boat
He is as gold as treasure
He is as cute as a cat
He is as sweet as a cherry
He is as slimy as a slug
His scales are as shiny as sparkly diamonds
He is Emily's goldfish.

Georgia Biggs (6)
Brambletye Preparatory School, East Grinstead

Untitled

It is as busy as a boarding school.
Its towers are as tall as giants.
It is as big as Iceland.
It is as exciting as a grand old castle.
It is as interesting as a death cap mushroom.
It is as much fun as a huge maze.
It is as lovely as a ruby red rose.
It is as cool as a roller coaster.
It is London.

Roland Bourne (7)
Brambletye Preparatory School, East Grinstead

Untitled

She is as pretty as a ruby rose.
She is as cheery as a cute puppy.
She is as sweet as sugar.
She is as glamorous as a show model.
She is as careful as a waitress.
She is as funny as a clown.
She sings as sweet as a robin.
She is Hannah Montana.

Ella Harrison (6)
Brambletye Preparatory School, East Grinstead

She Is . . .

She is as happy as a dog.
She is as funny as a monkey.
Her eyes are as brown as a teddy.
Her hair is as black as a bat.
She is as helpful as a mummy.
She dances as lovely as a fairy.
She is Mrs Lamb, my teacher.

Abigail Coleman (7)
Brambletye Preparatory School, East Grinstead

Untitled

He is as strong as a tiger
He is as fast as a cheetah
He is as prepared as a spitfire pilot
He is as skilful as a gymnast
He is as amazing as Superman
He is as famous as Michael Jackson
He is as clever as a scientist
He is Steven Gerrard.

Arthur Butt (7)
Brambletye Preparatory School, East Grinstead

Untitled

It is as clever as a scientist
It is as much fun as a slide
It is as gentle as a butterfly
It is as fast as a racing car
It is a dolphin.

Tallulah Haycock (6)
Brambletye Preparatory School, East Grinstead

Untitled

It is as clever as an elephant
It is as brave as a lion
It is as dark as the night
It is as scary as a skeleton
It is as furry as a platypus
It is as fast as a cheetah
It is as black as coal
It is as squeaky as a mouse
It is a bat.

Oskar Marten (6)
Brambletye Preparatory School, East Grinstead

My Friend Issy

She is as beautiful as a flower,
She is as sparkly as a crystal,
She is as glittery as a diamond,
She is as bonkers as a cake,
She is my friend, Issy.

Madeleine Roche (5)
Broad Hinton CE Primary School, Swindon

My Friend Madeleine

She's as cheeky as a monkey
She's as funny as a clown
She's as beautiful as sparkles
She's as pink as the sunset
She's as lovely as a petal
She's as clever as an adult
She's as gorgeous as glittery stars
She's as pretty as 100 crystals
She is better than Hannah Montana
She's as crazy as the wild animals
She's Madeleine Roche, my friend.

Issy Keen (6)
Broad Hinton CE Primary School, Swindon

Crazy Sister

She is as crazy as a wild animal
She is as small as a toilet
She loves black dragons
She is as light as a feather
She is as beautiful as a princess
She is my sister, Daisy.

Oliver Bromley (6)
Broad Hinton CE Primary School, Swindon

My Silly Sister

She is as annoying as a monkey,
She is as bouncy as a trampoline,
She is as funny as a chimpanzee,
She is as silly as a cat,
She is as beautiful as a cake,
She is my sister, Kelly.

Katie Harbottle (6)
Broad Hinton CE Primary School, Swindon

My Brother Is Called Max

He is as loud as a steam engine,
He is as playful as a cat,
He is as cute as a bear,
He is as cuddly as a dolphin,
He is my brother, Max.

Benjamin Philpott (5)
Broad Hinton CE Primary School, Swindon

Justin Bieber

He is as handsome as a Chihuahua,
He is as cute as Robbie Ray,
He is as good as children,
He is cooler than a dolphin,
He is hotter than Jason Derulo,
He is as bright as the sun,
He is more sparkly than the moon,
He is more funny than the teachers,
He is kinder than an adult,
He is Justin Bieber.

Eliza Hill (5)
Broad Hinton CE Primary School, Swindon

My Riddle

She is as beautiful as a flower,
She is as cool as a superstar,
She is as good as a star,
She is as sparkly as a crystal,
She is as big as a giant,
She is Hannah Montana.

Molly Powers (5)
Broad Hinton CE Primary School, Swindon

My Riddle

It is as funny as a clown,
It is as ferocious as a ferocious beast,
Its breath is as hot as lava,
It is as scary as your worst nightmare,
It is as green as grass,
It is as cheeky as a chimpanzee,
It is my pet dragon.

Charlie Blow (7)
Broad Hinton CE Primary School, Swindon

My Riddle

He is as fast as lightning
He is as bouncy as a bouncy ball
He is as great as a video game
He is better than a football
He is cooler than David Tennant
He is greater than the school
He is John Terry.

Michael Maslin (6)
Broad Hinton CE Primary School, Swindon

My Riddle

She is as fast as a cheetah,
She is as good at jumping as a ball,
She is as good at football as a football player,
She is as cute as a flower,
She is as young as 10 months old,
She is as fluffy as a cat,
She is as black as a black feather,
She is as loud as a farmer's tractor,
She is my puppy
Her name is Bramble.

Tilly Buxton (6)
Broad Hinton CE Primary School, Swindon

My Riddle

She is as cute as a flower,
She is as sparkly as a star,
She is as camouflaged as grass,
She is as light as a feather,
She is as fuzzy as a bush,
She is as fast as a rocket,
She is as squeaky as a mouse,
She is as wet as raindrops,
She is my cat, Willow!

Theodora Dellar (6)
Broad Hinton CE Primary School, Swindon

My Riddle

He's as serious as 007,
He's as scary as a T-rex,
He's as dangerous as a dragon,
He's as clever as a scientist,
He's as famous as the stars,
He's as awesome as Superman,
He is David Tennant.

Lawrence Iles (6)
Broad Hinton CE Primary School, Swindon

My First Riddle

She is as fluffy as a bear
She is as cute as a flower
She is as precious as a crystal
She is as white as a cloud
She is as cheeky as a chimp
She is as great as a princess
She is my pony called Rosie.

Georgina Pound (6)
Broad Hinton CE Primary School, Swindon

My Riddle

They are as naughty as a gorilla.
They are as sweet as sweets.
They are as cuddly as a bear.
They are as hungry as a rumbling tummy.
They are as shiny as a piece of tinfoil.
They are as cheeky as a monkey.
They are as beautiful as a crystal.
They are as small as a mouse.
They are my cats.

Lottie Quick (7)
Broad Hinton CE Primary School, Swindon

Fire

I am as hot as the sun
I crackle like a volcano
I make fluffy clouds
I am yellow and orange
I glow in the dark
I make everything warm and cosy
But don't touch me because I can burn you.

Iona Jane McTaggart (5)
Gravenhurst Lower School, Gravenhurst

Horse

I am as strong as an ox
I am as fast as the wind
I am as graceful as a ballerina
I am very big
I am very small
I am very brave
I run for my life
I have won wars
I have farmed lands
I have won competitions

I am a horse.

Abi Brown (6)
Gravenhurst Lower School, Gravenhurst

41

Tiger

I have stripes
But I am not a zebra
I have fur
I have sharp teeth.

Oliver Gunn (5)
Gravenhurst Lower School, Gravenhurst

Hoppity Hop

I am soft and cuddly
I have long ears and a fluffy tail
I like to hop and eat carrots
My house is called a burrow
I am a . . .

Amy Vass (5)
Gravenhurst Lower School, Gravenhurst

What Am I?

I am soft and furry
I have whiskers and four paws
I rhyme with mat
What am I?
A cat!

Sophie Thompson (5)
Gravenhurst Lower School, Gravenhurst

What Am I?

I have got sharp claws
I am brown
I have got fur not stripes
What am I?

Bear.

Ben Stone (6)
Gravenhurst Lower School, Gravenhurst

Guess Who?

I am nocturnal
I am furry
I like sunbathing
I have a black and white tail
I use my tail to help me climb
I like to eat fruit
I like to leap from tree to tree
I have a pointy nose
My name means ghost
I come from Madagascar
Who am I?
I am a lemur
My name is Billy.

Evie Bailey (6)
Gravenhurst Lower School, Gravenhurst

My Baby Sister

She is as fast as a rocket
She jumps around the house like a cricket
She is as talkative as a parrot
She makes me laugh when I'm sad.

Tyrik Afolabi (5)
Ilderton Primary School, London

Untitled

I am as big as a cat.
I am as small as a dog.
I am as round as a pig.
I am as good as a school.
I am as old as a house.
I am as tall as a tower.
I am as skinny as spaghetti.
I am as lovely as a butterfly.
I am as sweet as a lollipop.
I am as pretty as a princess.
Who am I?

Madyson Aka N'Guetta (5)
Ilderton Primary School, London

Auntie Sinita

She is as strict as a teacher,
She is as nice as a friend,
She is as cool as an ice lolly,
She is as tall as a tree,
She is as pretty as a princess,
She is Sinita, my auntie.

Harpreet Preeti Kaur (5)
Ilderton Primary School, London

Untitled

He is my best friend
He is different and he comes from Jamaica
He has Ben 10 towels and a book
He comes to my house
He plays Avatar games and Tom and Jerry
He has a DS
He is my friend, Jamal.

Champion Madubuko (6)
Ilderton Primary School, London

Rihanna

She's as beautiful as a butterfly.
She's got nice songs.
She wears a fantastic flowery dress.

She is Rihanna.

Mia Hinds (6)
Ilderton Primary School, London

Untitled

It's as fast as a lion,
It's as speedy as a chicken,
It's fast like a cheetah,
And it is a boy.

Romario Reid (6)
Ilderton Primary School, London

Untitled

It is as cute as a baby.
It is small.
It has a small nose.
It cries.
It has four feet.
It has paws.
It's as cute as Miss Moore.
It is a puppy.

Ayomide Ayeni (6)
Ilderton Primary School, London

He Can . . .

He can count.
He can ride a toy motorcycle.
He is very good at hiding.
He has a toy called Bunny.
He is my brother, Ahmad.

Hikmat Subuola Makinde (6)
Ilderton Primary School, London

Mirabel

She has lots of plaits.
She has two earrings.
She is wearing a skirt.
She is wearing boots.
She is as funny as a clown!
She has black eyes and black hair like the night.
She is six and a half.
She is my friend, Mirabel.

Aaliyah Rintoul (7)
Ilderton Primary School, London

Kick Buttowski

He's as fast as a horse.
He's better than a fire.
He's a daredevil as he can skateboard.
He likes being cool.
He's a big wrestler.
His friend is Gunther
And he is on Disney XD.
He is Kick Buttowski.

Soyemi David Olawale (6)
Ilderton Primary School, London

Untitled

She makes me laugh a lot.
And she plays with me.
And she likes me and my enormous sitter too.
She is the loveliest girl in the world.
She is my sister!

Mirabel Owusu (6)
Ilderton Primary School, London

Untitled

He is as cute as a fairy.
He loves my pencils.
He draws all over the place!
He loves playing catch.
He hugs his basket.
He loves bones.
He is my dog called Josh.

Amy Dembele (6)
Ilderton Primary School, London

Untitled

Sometimes he's faster than me,
He's like a brother to me,
He plays with me all the time!
He's my friend Luke.

La-Shane Dawkins-McLeod (7)
Ilderton Primary School, London

Rihanna

She is a singer
She dances well
She likes to sing
She is a fantastic person
She's Rihanna
She is wonderful.

Cheyenne Daley (6)
Ilderton Primary School, London

My Doll

She has white hair and she is mixed race
She has pink lipstick and has a sparkly pink dress
She is my doll.

Nissi Madubuko (6)
Ilderton Primary School, London

My Favourite Star

My favourite person,
She has long blonde hair,
She is Hannah Montana's friend
and she's very, very beautiful
and she's got the beauty at high school
and she's got two friends called Miley and Oliver.
Then she shouts a lot.
Then afterwards she's a nice girl.
She is Lilly Truscott.

Rachael Fatu Somah (6)
Ilderton Primary School, London

How Miss Jones Looks

She has brown hair,
She is a teacher,
She has plain hair,
The brown hair is long,
She has very light brown spots,
She has white coloured skin,
She has green eyes,
She has gold earrings today,
She is teaching 2D,
She is Miss Jones.

Emmanuel Adeniyi (7)
Ilderton Primary School, London

Riddle

He is as beautiful as a tiger
He is as scary as a dragon
He is 30 years old
He is younger than my mum
He is a slowcoach
He is my dad.

Lara Fateh (7)
Ilderton Primary School, London

Guess Who?

He has a necklace around his neck.
Gone to Deptford Green.
He used to be the fastest in Ilderton Primary School.
He is going to be 14 in November and he is going to get an iPod.
He has the same hair as me.
He plays the PlayStation a lot.
When I was 4 he was in year 6 and his class was 6L.
When I was 5 he was in year 7.
His bedroom is yellow with blue walls.
He is my brother.

Amahric Francis (6)
Ilderton Primary School, London

Untitled

She looks after my baby brother
She needs to do work on the computer all day
She is my mum.

Sahra Osman (6)
Ilderton Primary School, London

Gombardes

I have go karts
I have a big ball pit
I have a wobbly slide
I have a fantastic stair
I am Gombardes.

Darell Jones (6)
Ilderton Primary School, London

Untitled

He has floppy ears and a brown body
He eats carrots and lettuce
He has a little tail
He can jump
He is a rabbit.

Donis George (6)
Ilderton Primary School, London

The Teddy

Her eyes are blue.
I play with her.
I take her for a walk.
When she gets hungry, I feed her.
When it's time for bed, I put her to bed.
She is a teddy.

Rusherlee Blackwood (6)
Ilderton Primary School, London

My Riddles

I have got blue eyes and a bushy tail.
I've got four legs.
I am a dog.

I am very red.
People ride me.
I've got big windows and small windows.
I am a bus.

I'm grey and can change colour as well.
I eat flies.
I am a lizard.

Francesca Daly (6)
Ilderton Primary School, London

My Rabbit

I have pointed ears
I like carrots
I have a little bushy tail
People keep me as a pet
I hop and hop all the time
I'm white with pink in my ears
I have two teeth sticking out
I am a rabbit.

Nancy Payne (7)
Ilderton Primary School, London

This Is The Cat

It is furry
It licks its paws
It's first a kitten
It can be white and black
It gets chased by a boy
It's a cat.

Porscha Kent-Manzi (6)
Ilderton Primary School, London

Giraffe

I have four legs,
I have a long, long neck,
I have long legs,
I have short hair,
I am brown and cream,
I eat leaves,
I am a giraffe.

Zamin Mawjee (6)
Ilderton Primary School, London

The Teacher

She is a teacher,
She tells people off,
She has a sister,
She is very nice,
She has marbles in a jar,
She is Miss Jones.

Jadyn Green (6)
Ilderton Primary School, London

Grey Mouse Birthday

He is grey,
He has a pink tail,
His favourite food is cheese,
He is tiny,
He runs very fast,
He goes *squeak squeak,*
He has whiskers,
He is scary,
He comes in dirty houses,
He is a mouse.

Ayobami Abiodun Soluade (6)
Ilderton Primary School, London

My Giraffe

It has four legs and a long neck.
It is yellow and orange.
It eats leaves and grass.
It loves running every day.
It has ears and it is funny.
It has spots.
It has white teeth and they are shiny.
It has a baby girl.
It is a giraffe.

Taliyah McDonald (6)
Ilderton Primary School, London

Nice Striker

He is a good footballer,
He wants to quit,
He is in the newspapers,
He has got a picture in the newspaper,
He plays for England and Manchester United,
He is a skilled striker,
He once missed a match in Spain,
He has a wife that comes to every match he plays,
He also has a child,
He is Wayne Rooney.

Shadrach Gbenga-Ojo (7)
Ilderton Primary School, London

Who Is It?

She is as helpful as a friend.
She is as funny as a clown.
She is a good driver.
She is as pretty as a fairy.
She is cooler than a cucumber.
She is as fast as a cheetah.
She is my mummy.

Matthew Lewis (6)
Long Lane Primary School, Tilehurst

He Is . . .

He is as fast as a cheetah.
He is cool and kind.
He is as fantastic as a rock singer.
He is Liam.

Robert Lloyd (6)
Long Lane Primary School, Tilehurst

Untitled

He is as ugly as a troll
He is as strong as a monster
He is as clumsy as a bird
He is as slow as a kangaroo
He is Sam.

Saad Faisal (6)
Long Lane Primary School, Tilehurst

Who Is It?

She is as beautiful as her favourite colour.
She is as precious as a diamond.
She is as funny as a clown.
She is as helpful as a teacher.
She is my friend, Siena.

Amy Cannings (6)
Long Lane Primary School, Tilehurst

Untitled

He is as kind as a bird,
He is as bright as the sun,
He is great as a father,
He has a lot of hair,
He has freckles,
He is 24 years old,
He is as fast as a cheetah,
He has silver hair,
He is as tall as a giraffe
He scores a lot of goals
He is Wayne Rooney.

Louis Deasy (6)
Long Lane Primary School, Tilehurst

Who Is It?

He is as fast as a cheetah.
He is as clever as a hedgehog.
He is as smart as a president.
He is as grumpy as a rhino.
He is as cool as a pop star.
He is as light as a cat.
He is as bright as a star.
He is braver than a crocodile.
He is stronger than a wrestler.
He is as wonderful as a ghost, *wooo!*
He is as bright as a giraffe.
He can be as friendly as a bee.
He is as jolly as George.
He fights like a tiger.
He's the best person in the world!

Roshan Patel (7)
Long Lane Primary School, Tilehurst

Who Is It?

She is as funny as an animal
She is as pretty as a monkey
She is as lovely as a rainbow
She is as nice as a new car
She is as kind as a butterfly
She is as clever as a dog
She is Amy.

Siena Ramjug (6)
Long Lane Primary School, Tilehurst

Who Is It?

She is as good as gold
She is as funny as a clown
She is as bright as the sun
She is as jolly as a cat
She is as kind as a mummy
She is as clever as a kangaroo
She is as pretty as a princess
She is as precious as a diamond
She is nice like a butterfly
She is as happy as the stars
She is cuddly like a teddy
She is as cool as a freezer
She is jumpy like a frog
She is cold like snow.

Her name is Amy!

Caitlin Jugg (6)
Long Lane Primary School, Tilehurst

Who Is It?

He is as hot as a burning house
He is as scary as a dinosaur
He is as tiny as an ant
He is as fast as a tiger
He is as colourful as a rainbow
He is as sharp as a sword
He is as massive as a lion
He is Winter, my hamster.

Hayden Nunan (7)
Long Lane Primary School, Tilehurst

Who Is It?

She is as pretty as a rose
She is as funny as a game
She is as kind as a mum
She is as beautiful as a butterfly
She is as annoying as a frog
She is a silly as a mouse
She is as chatty as me
She is my sister, Leah.

Georgia Tolksdorf (6)
Long Lane Primary School, Tilehurst

Who Is It?

He is as hungry as a goat.
He is as big as a bus.
He is as hairless as a bone.
He is as funny as a clown.
He is as slow as a snail.
He is as strong as a stone.
He's my dad!

Luke Funnell (6)
Long Lane Primary School, Tilehurst

Who Is It?

She is as bright as a sun
She is as cute as a cat
She is as jolly as the queen
She is as beautiful as a butterfly
She is as kind as a dog
She is as tall as a tower
She is my friend, Phoebe!

Amelia Lee (6)
Long Lane Primary School, Tilehurst

Who Is It?

He is as clever as a teacher.
He is as bossy as a mum.
He is as funny as a clown.
He is as handsome as a man.
He is as sweaty as the sun.
He is as helpful as a servant.
He is fast at drinking his milk at school.
He is Siddharth, my brother.

Maya Jani (6)
Long Lane Primary School, Tilehurst

Who Is It?

She is as good as a dog,
She is as helpful as a neighbour,
She is as lovely as a cat,
She is as kind as a fairy,
She is as clever as a dad,
She is as funny as a slide,
She is as fast as me,
She is as beautiful as a butterfly,
She is as precious as my dad,
She is as bright as the sun,
She is as pretty as my sister.

She is my mum.

Jamie Everitt (6)
Long Lane Primary School, Tilehurst

She Is

She is as kind as a mummy.
She is as helpful as a schoolgirl.
She is as beautiful as a butterfly.
She is as cute as a princess.
She is as cuddly as a teddy.
She is as clever as a teacher.
She is as funny as a clown.
She is Amelia Lee.

Claudia Taylor (7)
Long Lane Primary School, Tilehurst

Guess Who?

She is as funny as a see-saw
She is as nice as a flower
She is as cute as a tasty cake
She is as precious as a rainbow
She is as fast as a racing car
She is a sparkly as the sun
She is as hot as the sun
She is Caitlin Crawley.

Georgina Burns (6)
Long Lane Primary School, Tilehurst

Who Is It?

He is as cool as Michael Jackson
He is as fast as a cheetah
He is a cool winger like Darren Fletcher
He is right-footed like me
He plays for Reading like Shane Long
He is as good as Cristiano Ronaldo
He is as strong as a boxer
He is as famous as Matisse
He is as shocking as all the football players
He is Hal Robson-Kanu.

Ben Callender (6)
Long Lane Primary School, Tilehurst

Guess Who?

She is as cool as an ice cream.
She is as clever as a teacher.
She is as nice as a butterfly.
She is as funny as a hedgehog.
She is as pretty as a rainbow.
She is as lovely as a diamond.
She is as cute as a dog.
She is my friend, Georgina.

Caitlin Crawley (7)
Long Lane Primary School, Tilehurst

Who Is It?

He is as clever as a teacher.
He is as kind as a mummy.
He is a good reader like Mrs Beddow.
He has good behaviour like my cousin.
He supports Manchester United like me.
He is my best friend.
He is as cool as a ghost.
He is as brave as a rock.
He is as nice as a cat.
He is my best friend, Louis Jack Deasy.

George Fairbairn (6)
Long Lane Primary School, Tilehurst

Who Is It?

He is handsome
He plays football like Steven Gerrard
He is as clever as a bird
He is as funny as a clown
He has a funny voice like a monkey.

Liam Mills (6)
Long Lane Primary School, Tilehurst

Who Is It?

He is faster than a cheetah
He is faster than a racing car
He is funnier than a clown
He is as cuddly as a baboon.

Riley Nunan (7)
Long Lane Primary School, Tilehurst

Untitled

He is as cute as a cat
He is as fast as a cheetah
He is as cool as an ice cream
He is as funny as a clown
He is Billy, my brother.

Molly-Ellen Gabriel (7)
Long Lane Primary School, Tilehurst

Who Is It?

He is as ugly as his mum
He is as rude as his dad
He is as tasty as a Coke
He is not as cool as the school
His friend is Mary
He is cheeky
He is not famous
He is as sharp as a car
He's not scary
He is jumpy
He is tiny

He is Tom.

Sam Jones (7)
Long Lane Primary School, Tilehurst

Guess Who?

She is as pretty as a flower
She is as kind as a fairy
She is as fast as a cheetah
She is as cuddly as a teddy

She is my mum.

Mia Simmonds (7)
Long Lane Primary School, Tilehurst

Guess Who?

He is as nice as a dog
He is as tall as a grown-up
He is as old and bony as a stick
He is a good cook.

Joshua Cadogan-Wilson (6)
Long Lane Primary School, Tilehurst

Guess Who?

She is as colourful as a beautiful butterfly
She is as scary as a ghost
She is as prickly as a hedgehog.

Chloe Bowyer (6)
Long Lane Primary School, Tilehurst

Who Is It?

He is as good as a ball.
He is as cool as a cat.
He is as fast as a racing car.
He is as helpful as a speck of magic dust.
He is as nice as a lion.

He is George.

Jack Taylor (7)
Long Lane Primary School, Tilehurst

Who Is It?

He is as cool as a freezer
He is as lovable as a robin
He is as famous as a model
He is as colourful as a rainbow
He is Justin Bieber.

Phoebe Hockey (7)
Long Lane Primary School, Tilehurst

What Is He?

He eats leaves
He has stripes
He is pretty
He is a zebra.

Lily Hauffe (5)
Midhurst CE Primary School, Midhurst

What Am I?

He is beautiful
He is as tall as a tree
He eats leaves
He can reach the clouds
He is a giraffe.

Lucie Shrives-Steele (5)
Midhurst CE Primary School, Midhurst

What Am I?

He is dangerous
He is groovy like a rock star
He is scary like a tiger
He is fierce like a cheetah
He is a lion.

Tatyana Blackman (6)
Midhurst CE Primary School, Midhurst

What Is He?

He is good
He is funny
He is cool
He is a shark.

Cameron McInally (5)
Midhurst CE Primary School, Midhurst

What Am I?

He is as hairy as a monkey
He is as big as a tree
He is as black as night
He likes leaves
He is a gorilla.

Nell Whitby (6)
Midhurst CE Primary School, Midhurst

What Am I?

He is loud
He has sharp teeth
He is as big as a car
He is a lion.

Luke Page (5)
Midhurst CE Primary School, Midhurst

What Am I?

He eats bananas
He swings on trees
He runs fast.

Jamie Duncton (5)
Midhurst CE Primary School, Midhurst

The Lion

He is as cool as a rock star
He is as hairy as bears
He is lovely
He is a lion.

Billy Lane (5)
Midhurst CE Primary School, Midhurst

What Is He?

He is as brown as a tree stump.
He is an excellent jumper.
He is excellent and very nice.
He is a gazelle.

Eve Daniels (6)
Midhurst CE Primary School, Midhurst

What Is He?

He is cheeky
He is hairy and long
He goes, 'Ooo-ee-ar!'
He jumps high
He is a monkey.

Joe Waldron (6)
Midhurst CE Primary School, Midhurst

What Is He?

He jumps really high
He has sharp horns
He has four hooves
He is a gazelle.

Oscar Rothwell (5)
Midhurst CE Primary School, Midhurst

Who Am I?

It is as big as a horse
It does make a loud noise
It is often white and brown in colour
It lives in a field
People love to drink its milk
It is a cow.

Dominic Merritt-Smith (6)
Midhurst CE Primary School, Midhurst

Who Am I?

It lives in South America.
It is as orange as the setting sun.
It is a member of the cat family.
It has a car named after it.
It moves like a flash of lightning.

Josh Slade (6)
Midhurst CE Primary School, Midhurst

What Am I?

It lives in the English countryside,
It lives in a hole in the ground or a cage,
It likes to eat carrots,
It has long, floppy ears,
It likes to be cuddled,
It is a rabbit.

Bradley Martin (6)
Midhurst CE Primary School, Midhurst

What Am I?

It is grey
It has big ears
It lives in a field
It eats grass
It makes a strange sound
People like to ride it on the back
It is a donkey.

Jake Williamson (7)
Midhurst CE Primary School, Midhurst

What Am I?

It is as furry as a mammoth
It lives in Africa.
It is as yellow as the sun.
It has a golden mane.

It's a lion.

Jack Burdon (6)
Midhurst CE Primary School, Midhurst

What Am I?

It is faster than an elephant.
It is put in a cage.
It runs about.
It sometimes lives in a house.
It is put into a cage.
It is small and fluffy.
It pushes a small ball.
It is a hamster.

Ollie Shaw (6)
Midhurst CE Primary School, Midhurst

Can You Guess The Animal?

I live in Africa.
I have black hooves.
I am as yellow as the sun.
I am taller than an ant but smaller than Big Ben.
I have brown squares all over me.
I am a giraffe.

Caitlin Crockford-Smith (7)
Midhurst CE Primary School, Midhurst

What Is It?

It lives in a hot country
It eats leaves and grass
Its body is yellow and brown
It is taller than a double decker bus
It has a long neck
It is a giraffe.

Abbie Laycock (6)
Midhurst CE Primary School, Midhurst

Who Is It?

It is bigger than a rabbit
but smaller than a giraffe.
It is as fierce as an angry person.
It can kill you.
It is faster than a chicken.
You can find it in zoos in England.
It is a panther.

Zaron Lane (6)
Midhurst CE Primary School, Midhurst

Who Am I?

It eats people
It has a mane
It can run as fast as a zebra
It eats meat
It is a lion.

Jack Court (6)
Midhurst CE Primary School, Midhurst

Dolphin

I am as smooth as a baby's bottom.
People ride on me.
I am a blue colour.

I can jump as high as a house.
I make a high squeaky noise.
I live in the cold ocean.
I am a dolphin.

Gemma Sansom (6)
Midhurst CE Primary School, Midhurst

What Is It?

It has orange skin like the sun.
It likes to eat meat.
It lives in Africa in the wild.
It lives in groups.
Its babies are called cubs.
It is a lion.

Amelia Field (6)
Midhurst CE Primary School, Midhurst

Who Is It?

It lives underwater.
It eats little fish.
It is as blue as the sky.
It squeaks to talk.
It is beautiful.
It is a dolphin.

Sophie Gamlin (6)
Midhurst CE Primary School, Midhurst

Who Is It?

It has got a long swishy tail
It can be white or brown
It likes to eat carrots
It lives in a field
Some people like to ride it
It is a horse.

Elize Heath (6)
Midhurst CE Primary School, Midhurst

Who Is It?

It is as yellow as the sun.
It is bigger than a meerkat
but smaller than an elephant.
It lives in Africa.
It runs like the wind.
It has a loud roar.
It has a mane.
It is a lion.

Eleni Georgiou (6)
Midhurst CE Primary School, Midhurst

My Dad

He is as fast as a dog
He is as strong as a giant
He is as clever as a teacher
He is as happy as sunshine
He is as funny as a clown
He is a dad.

Mitchell Shirley (6)
Queensway School, Banbury

My Teacher

He is as tall as a tree
He is as kind as a teacher
He has a badge but not a birthday badge
He is Mr Cusden, my teacher.

Alishba Farooq (7)
Queensway School, Banbury

My Mummy

She is as beautiful as Lindsey.
She is as strong as Daddy.
She is as clever as me.
She is as funny as a clown.
She is as fast as a cheetah.
She is my mummy.

Jessica Wilson (7)
Queensway School, Banbury

My Friend, Zoe

She is as sweet as a cake.
She is as pretty as a humming bird.
She is as funny as a clown.
She is as beautiful as a butterfly.
She is as fun as a party.
She is Zoe, my friend.

Ella Prior (7)
Queensway School, Banbury

Untitled

Mum is as cuddly as a dog
Mum is as warm as a scarf
Mum is as strong as a lorry
Mum is as lovely as a flower
Mum is as kissy as a dog
My mum is a person.

George Theakston (7)
Queensway School, Banbury

Cheetah

He is as fast as a lion
He is as spotty as a dog
He is as yellow as the sun
He is as strong as a lion
He is as big as a clock
He is a cheetah.

Oliver Molski (7)
Queensway School, Banbury

Untitled

Dad is as funny as a monkey
He is as strong as a bear
He is as big as a tree
He is as fast as a tiger
He is a dad.

Angel Alderman (7)
Queensway School, Banbury

My Brother Louis

He is as funny as a joke
He is as fast as a cheetah
He is as cool as a T-shirt
He is as clever as a car
He is as cuddly as a sheep
He is my brother, Louis.

Jamie O'Rourke (6)
Queensway School, Banbury

My Mummy

She is as beautiful as a flower
She is as fast as a cheetah
She is as big as a door
She is as strong as an elephant
She is as cuddly as a bear
She is a lovely person.

Holly Belcher (6)
Queensway School, Banbury

Steven Gerrard

He loves football.
His friends help him.
He supports Liverpool and England.
He loves his coach very much.
He is Steven Gerrard.

Ellie Jones (6)
Queensway School, Banbury

All About Me

She is as happy as a smile
She is as beautiful as a flower
She is as clever as a scientist
She is as fast as a cheetah
She is as good as a firefighter
She is me, Abi.

Abigail Gough (6)
Queensway School, Banbury

He Is

He is as fast as a cheetah.
He is as funny as a joke.
He is as strong as a lion.
He is as big as a giant.
He is as happy as a smiley face.
He is my daddy.

Zoe Mandeman (6)
Queensway School, Banbury

Mummy

She is as funny as a joke.
She is as happy as a monkey.
She is as cuddly as a bear.
She is as beautiful as a tulip.
She is as big as a giant.
She is my mum.

Egan Moore (6)
Queensway School, Banbury

My Pop Star

He is as great as a monkey.
He is good at singing like Hannah Montana.
He is super at dancing like Emily Osment.
He is as kind as my mum.
He is Michael Jackson.

Rana El Hassan (6)
Queensway School, Banbury

My Dad

He is as funny as a dog.
He is as strong as a panda.
He is as fast as a cheetah.
He is as clever as a fish.
He is as happy as a flower.
He is my dad.

Joshua Clarke (6)
Queensway School, Banbury

Birthday Cake

It is as chocolatey as a sweet
It is as smelly as a sock
It has five candles
It is a cake.

James Coles (6)
Queensway School, Banbury

My Mum

She is as beautiful as a bride.
She has very nice clothes.
She is the best mum.
She is kind, that is why I love her.
She has a house and I love it.
She is my mum.

Lana El Hassan (6)
Queensway School, Banbury

Mum

She is as kind as a firefighter.
She is as happy as a monkey.
She is as beautiful as a butterfly.
She is as funny as a clown.
She is as mad as a tiger.
She is my mum.

Megan Hawtin (6)
Queensway School, Banbury

My Friend, Chelsea

She is as kind as a nurse.
She is as strong as a dinosaur.
She is as mad as a monkey.
She is as naughty as a lion.
She is as happy as a smiley face.
She is Chelsea, my friend.

Amir Fellah (6)
Queensway School, Banbury

Mummy

She is as happy as a flower.
She is as beautiful as a butterfly.
She is as slow as a snail.
She is as kind as a dad.
She is as funny as a clown.
She is my mum.

Josie Munoz (6)
Queensway School, Banbury

Crunchy And Sweet

It is orange and sweet, small
It is crunchy and hard, munchy
It is juicy and thin, long
It is cold and it has five leaves on the top
It is thick, it has a flat side on the bottom
It is a carrot
It is like a tasty apple
You can make carrot juice
You can break it
You can take the leaves off
They have five leaves on the top.

Jerom Kaantharasan (7)
St Francis Catholic Primary School, Stratford

The Juicy Apple

What am I?
I am red and round and juicy,
I have a short brown stem,
I am green and red and crunchy,
I'm yummy and sweet,
I look like the Earth,
I make juice if you squeeze me,
I am as juicy as an orange,
You can mix me with fruit juice,
I am a sweet juicy apple.

Querida Addo (6)
St Francis Catholic Primary School, Stratford

What Am I?

What am I?
He is small.
He has big cheeks.
He can stand up.
He can talk.
I am a baby.

Cameron Laronde (6)
St Francis Catholic Primary School, Stratford

It Is A Juicy Apple

What am I?
It's round, nice, juicy and crunchy,
It's nice and red and green and fresh,
It's got a couple of seeds,
It is a middle size fruit,
It makes juice,
My mum says I should have five a day,
I am an apple!

Prince-Manuel Commodore (7)
St Francis Catholic Primary School, Stratford

Untitled

He's got soft blond hair,
He's a good friend,
He's white,
He's got soft skin,
He's from Poland,
He's a very good student,
Who is he?

Julia Dajczer (7)
St Francis Catholic Primary School, Stratford

99

Who Is He?

He is as helpful as a butterfly
He is as nice as a reindeer
He is as strong as a house
He is my brother.

Malachi Oduro (5)
St Francis Catholic Primary School, Stratford

Untitled

She is as pretty as a princess.
She is as lovely as a castle.
She is as friendly as a puppy.
She is Natalia.

Artur Baran (5)
St Francis Catholic Primary School, Stratford

Untitled

She is as pretty as a princess
She is as tall as a building
She is as beautiful as a flower
She is Mum.

Gabrielle Denkyirah (5)
St Francis Catholic Primary School, Stratford

He Is

He is as fluffy as a grandma's hair.
He is as beautiful as a king.
He is as tall as a building.
He is Elvin.

Lucrenzia Ampomah (5)
St Francis Catholic Primary School, Stratford

Untitled

He is as furry as a bear
He is as wicked as a DJ
He is as small as a mouse
He is Owen.

Keandre Da Silva (5)
St Francis Catholic Primary School, Stratford

Untitled

She is as pretty as a princess
She is as tall as a tower
She is as funny as a clown
She is fun
She is my mum.

Zoe Citalois (5)
St Francis Catholic Primary School, Stratford

Untitled

He is as small as a fish.
He is as brave as a cheetah.
He is as young as a puppy.
He is Ben 10.

William Rabuya (5)
St Francis Catholic Primary School, Stratford

Untitled

He is as fierce as a lion.
He is as soft as a pillow.
He is as mad as a tiger.
He is Alex, my brother.

Nicholas Kandratsenka (5)
St Francis Catholic Primary School, Stratford

Barbie

She is pretty like a flower.
She is soft like a rabbit.
She is kind like a kid.
She is Mama.

Andria Benny (5)
St Francis Catholic Primary School, Stratford

Daddy

He is nice to me like my teddy.
He is funny like me.
He is kind like a ladybird.
He is strong.

Cyrus Harewood (5)
St Francis Catholic Primary School, Stratford

Untitled

He is as strong as a castle.
He is as nice as a king.
He is as pretty as a flower.
He is Fabio Capello.

Rocco Dichio (5)
St Francis Catholic Primary School, Stratford

Teddy Bear

He is as soft as wool.
He is as furry as a feather.
He is as good as a rainbow.
He is Teddy Bear.

Chinedu Elo-Chikezie (6)
St Francis Catholic Primary School, Stratford

She Is

She is as funny as a clown.
She is as soft as a pillow.
She is as cuddly as a koala.
She is Mum.

Daisy Plante (5)
St Francis Catholic Primary School, Stratford

Untitled

She is as pretty as a princess.
She is as good as a sunny day.
She is as helpful as a mum.
She is Yvonne, my sister.

Ngozi Ogike (5)
St Francis Catholic Primary School, Stratford

Uhsr

He is as funny as a clown.
He is as tall as a giant.
He is as nice as a mum.
He is Uhsr.

Nana Akyeaw (5)
St Francis Catholic Primary School, Stratford

Ben 10

He is powerful like a king
He is brave like a lion
He is good like a kid
He is super like a hero

He is Ben 10.

Joacquin Paulo (5)
St Francis Catholic Primary School, Stratford

Untitled

It's crunchy, raw and juicy,
It's green and red,
It's sweet and round,
It's hard and soft,
It's scrummy and it's OK.

Ellicia Okanju (6)
St Francis Catholic Primary School, Stratford

Mr Kiernan

He is a good teacher and as good as a king.
He is amazing like a clown.
He is good and very kind.

Ivana Morgan (5)
St Francis Catholic Primary School, Stratford

Ben 10

He is like a king
He is like a clown
He is like a brave man
He is Ben 10.

Oluwatamilore Alegbe (5)
St Francis Catholic Primary School, Stratford

Stephanie

She is friendly like a princess
She is polite like my mum
She is pretty like a fairy
She is lovely.

Emely Pilaquinga Freeman (5)
St Francis Catholic Primary School, Stratford

Harmony

She is lovely like Barbie girl is lovely.
She is like a princess because
Harmony is a princess.
She is the best in the world.

She is Harmony.

Olamojiba Joseph (5)
St Francis Catholic Primary School, Stratford

My Friend Andria

She is cute like a cat.
She is soft like a blanket.
She is funny like a clown.
She is Andria.

Motunrayo Olulode (5)
St Francis Catholic Primary School, Stratford

Ivana

Ivana, she is beautiful like a princess.
She is cute like a Barbie doll.
She is as friendly as a dolphin.

Joshua Nunes Silva (5)
St Francis Catholic Primary School, Stratford

Selena Gomez

She is as nice as a bunny.
She is as smart as a teacher.
She is as happy as Darren.
She is as funny as my mum and dad.
She is as rich as Simon Cowell.
She is as cute as Mrs Peng.
She is as big as a child.
She is Selena Gomez.

Bryana Findlay (6)
St Francis Catholic Primary School, Stratford

Wayne Rooney

He is as strong as a lion.
He is as rich as gold.
He is as cool as a cucumber.
He plays for Manchester United.
He is as brave as a dragon.
He is number 9.
He is as fast as a motorbike.
He is as famous as Simon Cowell.
He is as skilful as Ronaldo.
He is forward in Manchester.
He is Wayne Rooney.

Toju Edomi (6)
St Francis Catholic Primary School, Stratford

Elvis Presley

He is as famous as Simon Cowell.
He is as fast as an Audi and a Ferrari.
He is as rich as a king.
He is as cool as a cucumber.
He is Elvis Presley.

Ethan Suppaya Palomino (6)
St Francis Catholic Primary School, Stratford

Katy Perry

She is as popular as a flower
She is as rich as a queen
She is as pretty as a princess
She is as gorgeous as a cat
She is as lovely as a flower
She is as famous as a home
She is as beautiful as a monster
She is Katie Perry.

Georgina Odunsi (6)
St Francis Catholic Primary School, Stratford

Harry Potter

He is as strong as a dragon
He is as rich as Simon
He is as mean as Simon
He is as cool as a ray
He is as big as a lion
He is Harry Potter.

Devonte Lambert (6)
St Francis Catholic Primary School, Stratford

Katy Perry

She is as pretty as a princess
She is as gorgeous as a popstar girl.
She is a flower and a pretty girl.
She is a lovely girl.
She is Katy Perry.

Helen-Jade Abbey (7)
St Francis Catholic Primary School, Stratford

Michael Jackson

He is strong like a gorilla.
He is as popular as a rock star.
He is as cool as a pop star.
He is as mean as a man.
He is a king as a friend.
He is as cute as a cat.
He is as popular as a rock star.
He is nice as a friend.
He is as happy as a kitten.
He is Michael Jackson.

Osazuwa David (6)
St Francis Catholic Primary School, Stratford

John Terry

He is stronger than a dog.
He is as cool as a rock star.
He is as rich as a king.
He is as talented as a tiger.
He is smarter than Simon.
He is more famous than me.
He smells nice.
He is nice.
He is John Terry.

Gerard Cosmo Jarrett (6)
St Francis Catholic Primary School, Stratford

Simon Cowell

He's as mean as a monster.
He's as rich as a king.
He's as fast as a racing car.
He's as cool as a black car.
He's as wicked as a witch.
He's as strong as a giant.
He's as nice as a teacher.
He is Simon Cowell.

Darren Barbeki (7)
St Francis Catholic Primary School, Stratford

Cheryl Cole

She is as pretty as a kitty.
She is as fancy as a princess.
She sings like a girl.
She's as fabulous as a diamond.
She's like a kitty.
She is rich.
She is Cheryl Cole.

Angel Evboren (6)
St Francis Catholic Primary School, Stratford

Harry Potter

He is as famous as Michael Jackson
He is as funny as a clown
He is as medium as a worm
He is as wicked as a witch
He is as happy as people
He is as cool as a star
He is as nice as a friend
He is as handsome as a teacher
He is as magical as a wizard
He is as good as children

He is Harry Potter.

Jazmyn Cabey (6)
St Francis Catholic Primary School, Stratford

Amanda

She is as cute as a flower.
She is as pretty as a kitten.
She is as fashionable as a puppy.
She is as sweet as a rainbow.
She is as nice as a model.
She is beautiful and lovely.
She is Amanda.

Nkechi Onyido (6)
St Francis Catholic Primary School, Stratford

A White Fluffy Kitten

She is as cute as a butterfly,
She is as pretty as a diamond.
She is as smooth as a cloth.
She is as fluffy as a feather.
She is as cool as a pop star.
She is as lovely as a flower.
She is as soft as a bed.
She is as playful as a baby.
She is as famous as a star.
A white fluffy kitten.

Adrianna Jakubowska (6)
St Francis Catholic Primary School, Stratford

Frank Lampard

He is as fast as a Ferrari.
He is as quiet as a kitten.
He is as cool as a cucumber.
He is as rich as a rich man.
He is handsome.
He is as rude as a troll.
He is Frank Lampard.

Emmanuel Poku (6)
St Francis Catholic Primary School, Stratford

Harry Potter

He is as brilliant as a fish.
He is as magical as a diamond.
He is as happy as a boy.
He is as famous as Simon Cowell.
He dances like a ballet dancer.
He is Harry Potter.

Liam Duggan (6)
St Francis Catholic Primary School, Stratford

What Am I?

I am juicy like an orange,
Hard and red like a red cup,
Sweet and green like a green lemon,
Round and green like a green circle,
Red and green as a red and green circle,
I am an apple.

Pascal Marimootoo (6)
St Francis Catholic Primary School, Stratford

Good Juicy Apple

This is red and juicy!
It is nice crunchy and sweet!
You can have milkshake with it!
It loves to cheer people up.
It's an apple.

Atinuke Lucretia Fakunle (6)
St Francis Catholic Primary School, Stratford

My Riddle

Big as a tiger,
Funny as a clown,
Lovely as a mum,
Annoying as a football,
Good as a girl,

It is my brother.

Reshaé Nathaniel-Ridge (6)
St John's CE Walham Green Primary School, Fulham

My Riddle

He is as greedy as a pig,
He is as funny as a clown,
He is as pesty as a dog coming up to us and annoying us,
He is as blond as a rabbit.

Oliver Loveland-Jones
St John's CE Walham Green Primary School, Fulham

My Riddle

She is as squeaky as a baby,
She's as black as the night,
Her nose is as wet as a raindrop,
She is as good as a mouse,
She's as noisy as a dog,
She is my cat.

Harvey Adams (6)
St John's CE Walham Green Primary School, Fulham

My Riddle

As sweet as a chocolate
She is as beautiful as a butterfly
She is as honest as Santa
As cute as a cat
As lovely as a fairy
It is Miss Wigan.

Mia Tickel (6)
St John's CE Walham Green Primary School, Fulham

My Riddle

As healthy as an eagle
As fast as a cheetah
As funny as a clown
He is as tall as a tree
He is 6 feet tall like a dinosaur
He is as strong as a gorilla
He is as wise as an Egyptian
He is as kind as a puppy
He is as friendly as a dog.

Michael.

Joseph Vilone (7)
St John's CE Walham Green Primary School, Fulham

My Riddle

She's as cuddly as a bear.
She's as sleepy as a bunny.
She's as grey as a hamster.
She's as snugly as a monkey.
She has a pink top.
She's as fluffy as a chick.
She's as lovely as a bunny.
She's as soft as a cat,
She's as big as a bear.
She's as cute as a cat.
She is a teddy.

Elona Hoxha (6)
St John's CE Walham Green Primary School, Fulham

My Riddle

As small as a mouse.
As funny as a parrot.
As scary as a bear.
As clever as a cheetah.
As cool as a pop star.
As beautiful as a bride.
As scruffy as a parrot.
As kind as a mother.
As cheeky as a bird.
As cunning as a dad.
It is my sister.

Jessica Standring (7)
St John's CE Walham Green Primary School, Fulham

My Riddle

As healthy as a swimmer,
As nice as a fairy,
As funny as a clown,
As lovely as a butterfly,
As wise as a wizard,
As beautiful as a flower,
As fast as a car,
As grateful as the sun,
As sharing as a fish,
As strong as a rock,
As magic as a wizard,
As kind as a unicorn,
As brave as a snake.

Tara Aglionby (7)
St John's CE Walham Green Primary School, Fulham

My Riddle

She is as honest as Santa,
She is as lovely as a unicorn,
Helpful as a flower,
She is as good as a teddy,
She is as kind as a fairy,
She is as nice as a butterfly,
She is Miss Wigan.

Chloe Fleming (6)
St John's CE Walham Green Primary School, Fulham

My Riddle

As cute as a unicorn
It is as smelly as a puppy
It is as good as your big brother
It is as fluffy as a dog
It is as beautiful as the fair
It has shiny eyes
It is very soft
It is very cuddly
It is small
It is very furry
It is a teddy.

Ciann Pearman-Goodlitt (7)
St John's CE Walham Green Primary School, Fulham

My Riddle

He is as funny as a wobbly apple.
He is as tall as a pylon.
He is as great as my friends.
He is my dad.

Max Hirons (6)
St John's CE Walham Green Primary School, Fulham

My Riddle

He's as sweet as a puppy,
His nose is as wet as a raindrop,
He's as funny as a dog,
He's sleepy in the mornings,
He's strong and brave like a fireman,
He's got a family,
He's got spots on him,
He's got two children,
He's as nice as a butterfly,
He's got a long tail,
He's got a smile on his face every day!
He's happy,
He is a puppy.

Kian Reeves (6)
St John's CE Walham Green Primary School, Fulham

My Riddle

She is as pretty as a unicorn,
She is as funny as a monkey,
She is as lucky as a cat,
She is as cuddly as a bunny,
She is as sweet as candy,
She is a dog.

Amber Smyth (7)
St John's CE Walham Green Primary School, Fulham

Bowser

He goes in shooting,
He is a scary giant,
Spiky, greedy, hey!
As gigantic as a dinosaur,
He is Bowser.

Harry Giles (6)
St John's CE Walham Green Primary School, Fulham

My Riddle

His nose is as wet as a wolf's,
He is as sweet as a cat,
He is as white as a ghost,
He is as harmless as a little boy,
He is my dog.

Freddie Sweeney (6)
St John's CE Walham Green Primary School, Fulham

My Riddle

He is stronger than T-rex.
He breathes fire.
He has a spiky shell.
He is giant.
He is as bad as a giant.
He is Bowser.

Alfie Michael Richardson-Graves (7)
St John's CE Walham Green Primary School, Fulham

Riddles

He's as amazing as Diversity,
He's as talented as Flawless,
He's as original as sweeties,
He's as strong as a tiger,
He's as famous as a sculpture,
He's as cool as ice,
He's as nice as a cuddly bear,
He's George Sampson.

Remior Williams (7)
St John The Divine CE Primary School, London

Riddles

He is as nice as an ice cream,
He is as good as the sun,
He is as short as a dwarf,
He is as cute as a kitten,
He is as talented as a fish,
He is as silly as a brat,
He is as handsome as a peacock,
He is as funny as a clown,
He is Samel.

Dara Owolabi (6)
St John The Divine CE Primary School, London

Riddles

She's as amazing as Hannah Montana,
She's as famous as Alicia Keys,
She's as chubby as Santa Claus,
She's a model like Pixie Lott,
She's as sweet as a cherry,
She's as beautiful as a flower,
She's as cute as a kitten,
She's as popular as a film star,
She's as girly as a model,
She's as pretty as a butterfly,
She's Cheryl Cole.

Blessed Olowolagba (7)
St John The Divine CE Primary School, London

Riddles

He is as clever as a boy,
He is as kind as a girl,
He is as smart as Santa Claus,
He is as handsome as a prince,
He is as good as a man,
He is as intelligent as a teacher,
He is as famous as a Ferris wheel,
He is Kipper.

Yaaseen Miah (6)
St John The Divine CE Primary School, London

Riddles

She is as happy as a dog,
She is as silly as a chimpanzee,
She is as friendly as a horse,
She is as normal as a zebra,
She is as sleepy as a pig,
She is as funny as a monkey,
She is as truthful as a tortoise,
She is as sweet as a peach,
She is as clever as a spider,
She is as pretty as a bridesmaid,
She is as intelligent as a lion,
She is my Aunt Helen.

Jennifer Peters (7)
St John The Divine CE Primary School, London

Riddles

He is as lazy as a pig,
He is as selfish as a baby,
He is as tricky as a snake,
He is as clever as a spider,
He is as greedy as a monkey,
He is as famous as Michael Jackson,
He is Anansi.

Chi Ennis McLean (6)
St John The Divine CE Primary School, London

Riddles

She is as famous as Usain Bolt,
She is as amazing as Hannah Montana,
She is as pretty as a flower,
She is as kind as a princess,
She is as cute as a kitten,
She is as nice as Demi Lovato,
She is as lovely as the sun,
She is as popular as Alicia Keys,
She is as sweet as a cherry,
She is as cool as a DJ,
She is as beautiful as a butterfly,
She is Cheryl Cole.

Jessica Kesse (10)
St John The Divine CE Primary School, London

Animal Riddle

I have two legs.
I like to sit on a branch.
I only come out at night-time.
I have claws and feathers.
I love living in the trees.
What am I?
Owl.

William Addison, Iris Murphy, Thomas Pearson, Eli Price & Holly Record (5/6)
St Peter's CE Infant School, Tandridge

The Hole

The more I take away the bigger I get.
If you go too far I'll get wet.
I may be here today and not tomorrow.
Children play inside me.
I can be anywhere around you.
You'd better watch out for me in a road.
I'm a hole.

Francesca Riley (7)
St Peter's CE Infant School, Tandridge

The Swinging Flame

My favourite food is fruit,
I sometimes live in a zoo,
Sometimes I live in the wild,
I swing through the trees,
My fur is the colour of dark flames,
I love to play and be cheeky,
Can you guess who I am?

I am an orang-utan.

Eleanor Staples (6)
St Peter's CE Infant School, Tandridge

The Just So Stories By Rudyard Kipling

O best beloved . . .
I am as curious as a cat,
Fascinating as a bat,
Interesting as a scientist,
Fantastic as Mr Fox,
Extraordinary as Matilda,
Magical as a wizard,
Great as God,
Good as the Good King,
Exciting as going to the museum,
Odd as a number and strange as an alien,
What am I?

Leon Stefanopoulos (7)
St Peter's CE Infant School, Tandridge

Millipede

My legs are green.
I am not an insect.
I can have over a hundred legs.
I am not harmful.
What am I?

Christopher Green (6)
St Peter's CE Infant School, Tandridge

Black Cat

I have four paws and a furry coat.
I was worshipped in Ancient Egypt.
I can jump five times as high as my tail.
A group of us is called a clowder.
I have big ears.
I can see in colour.
I eat mice.
I say miaow.
What am I?

Francesca Beattie (6)
St Peter's CE Infant School, Tandridge

My Dog

It sometimes attacks
They are usually brown
They have lots of colours
They sometimes help people
It lives in a kennel
What is it?
It is my dog.

Matthew Clarke (6)
St Peter's CE Infant School, Tandridge

What Am I?

I am like a car but smaller.
I have an engine that uses petrol.
I have four wheels like a car, but smaller.
I have no roof or windows.
You ride me on and off the road.
What am I?

Jamie Stolton (7)
St Peter's CE Infant School, Tandridge

Sunny Garden

I am hard like an apple
I am orange
I have a green bit on the top
When you eat me, I am crunchy
What am I?

Emily Amy Ely (6)
St Peter's CE Infant School, Tandridge

As White As . . .

I am cold, soft and light
and I fall day or night
I can cover all the ground
and you can roll me round and round
When it's hot I go away
and come back on a winter day.

Sophie Williams (6)
St Peter's CE Infant School, Tandridge

Boa Constrictor

It is as pretty as a flower
It looks like a button you press
It is as slippery as a slug
Its teeth are as sharp as a crocodile's teeth
It is a boa constrictor.

Hamish Bignell, Emma Stocker, Edward Modra, Bella Brazier, Olivia
Cholerton & Jake Neaves (4/5)
St Peter's CE Infant School, Tandridge

Green Frog

He is as green as the grass
His eyes are blue like water
He is smooth like a smoothie
His tongue is red like a bus
He is a green frog.

Lewis Gould, William Nockles, Amber Gillespie, James Richards & Lily Stefanopoulos (4/5)
St Peter's CE Infant School, Tandridge

Peacock

It has ticklish feathers like a bird
It has spots like a boa constrictor
It is as green as a grasshopper
It opens up like a colourful flower
It is a peacock.

Rosa Grayling, Peter Lenihan, Saskia Bignell, Jenson Seal & Myles Jarrott-Chase (4/5)
St Peter's CE Infant School, Tandridge

White Dog

He has a yellow collar
He has teeth as sharp as a dinosaur's
He is as white as snow
His paws are as brown as a wolf
He is a white dog.

**Daniel Brown, Millie Bullock, Thomas Higgins, Lily Basset, Nikolai Choat &
Fred Webzell (4/5)**
St Peter's CE Infant School, Tandridge

Yellow Duck

He is yellow like the sun
His feathers are soft like a cushion
His webbed feet are pink like a pig
His beak is hard like a log
He is a yellow duck.

**Laura Bickerstaff, Freddie Forkan, Lucy Louden, Angelina Bartholomeou,
Alaisdair Evans & Alex Topping (4/5)**
St Peter's CE Infant School, Tandridge

Tasty Riddle

I look like an acorn
I feel hard and squidgy
I taste like jelly
I smell like jam
I am a grape.

Lenny Senior (6)
The Meads Primary School, East Grinstead

What Am I?

I look like a thistle sticking out of a bush
I feel like a hedgehog curled up
I taste bitter and sweet at the same time
I smell like sherbet, fresh as the morning air
I am a pineapple.

Jamie Stoner (6)
The Meads Primary School, East Grinstead

What Am I?

I look like a big hairy grape
I feel very furry but rough
I taste fizzy like a fizzy drink
I smell like a juicy apple
I am a kiwi.

Ben Paulwell (6)
The Meads Primary School, East Grinstead

What Am I?

I look like a tiny red or green egg.
Inside I feel as slippery as a brown slug
Inside I am sweet but my skin tastes sour
I smell of nothing until you bite into me
I am some grapes.

Jessica Aylen (6)
The Meads Primary School, East Grinstead

What Am I?

I look like an upside down rocket that has fire coming out.
I feel as spiky as a cactus.
I taste like exploding jelly that can be sweet and sour
And I smell as juicy as a grape.

I am a pineapple.

Hannah Sisley (6)
The Meads Primary School, East Grinstead

What Am I?

I look like a cactus
I feel as spiky as a palm tree
I taste juicy and mouth watering
I smell as sweet as my favourite sweet
I am a pineapple.

Luke Peel (6)
The Meads Primary School, East Grinstead

What Am I?

I look like a massive acorn when I am green.
Outside I feel smooth like ice.
Inside I taste sweet and juicy.
I smell like some juice in a glass.
I grow on a twisting vine.
I am a grape.

Eleanor Lacey (6)
The Meads Primary School, East Grinstead

What Am I?

I feel like a green tennis ball being hit across the court.
I look like a chicken's egg being laid by a fat chicken
And I am green like grass being trodden on in the park.
I taste fresh and sweet like a traffic light lolly on a hot day.
I smell sour like a sour sweet being sucked by a child.
I am from a tree in a hot country.
I am a kiwi.

Emily Williams (6)
The Meads Primary School, East Grinstead

What Am I?

I feel smooth like a colourful photograph hanging from the wall.
I taste sweet like chocolate buttons that melt in your mouth.
I look like a bouncy ball.
I smell sweet like pineapple.
My favourite place to be is at the top of the tree in hot countries.

I am a pomegranate.

Leah Bowley (6)
The Meads Primary School, East Grinstead

What Am I?

I am as bushy as a dark green apple tree in a light green spiky field.
I am heavy when I carry a big bag on my shoulders
when I move house.
I taste a bit sweet like a sour sweetie in my yummy tummy.
You will find me in a green and brown garden.
I am broccoli.

Olivia Ody (6)
The Meads Primary School, East Grinstead

What Am I?

I feel smooth like a piece of silver foil covering left-overs.
I taste squishy like a yellow sponge cake.
I look thin like a dolphin's fin as it dives into the deep blue water.
I smell like a little round green mint.
You will find me on a green plant growing in the dark soil.
I am a pea pod.

Oliver Jeffries (6)
The Meads Primary School, East Grinstead

What Am I?

I am as sharp as a needle.
I taste like a chewy bit of chewing gum.
I smell like a fresh Galaxy bar being squished on someone's skin.
I look like a honeycomb being made by buzzing bees.
You will find me on palm trees in Spain.
I am a pineapple.

Oliver Ally (6)
The Meads Primary School, East Grinstead

What Am I?

I feel smooth like a shiny red ball being juggled in a crowded circus.
I look like a creamy white pearl in a peach clam in
the deep ocean but I'm purple like Ribena.
I taste like a freshly baked sugary doughnut.
I smell like honey dripping from the beehives
in the beekeeper's green field.
I grow in rainy and sunny countries.
I am a plum.

Sophie Taylor (7)
The Meads Primary School, East Grinstead

What Am I?

I'm curved like a boomerang up high in the midday sky.
I feel like a piece of cold lead.
I taste like a cosy yellow teddy bear.
A hungry child will come looking for me soon.
I am a banana.

Reiss Wright (7)
The Meads Primary School, East Grinstead

What Am I?

I look like the evening sun.
I feel like a dragon's tooth gleaming like mad.
I taste like a crunchy rocket firing down your throat.
I smell like a bucket of fresh water.
I grow in the ground.
I'm as orange as the middle of a traffic light.
I'm a carrot.

Thomas Barham (6)
The Meads Primary School, East Grinstead

A Pomegranate

It's as red as an apple
It's as hard as a table
It's as round as a ball.

Jake Hodges (5)
The Meads Primary School, East Grinstead

A Kiwi

It's as green as the grass.
It's as soggy as a wet tissue.
It's as furry as a squirrel.

Layla Cowley (5)
The Meads Primary School, East Grinstead

A Grape

It is as juicy as a Starburst.
As soft as orange jam.
It is as smooth as a piece of paper.
It is green like a frog.
What is it?

Emie Edwards (6)
The Meads Primary School, East Grinstead

A Pineapple

It is as spiky as a Venus Flytrap
It is as juicy as grass
It is as yellow as the sun
It has smooth leaves
What is it?

Katie Murphy (6)
The Meads Primary School, East Grinstead

A Kiwi

It is as green as a bush.
It is as fizzy as a bottle of fizzy water.
It is as hairy as a dog.
It is as slimy as a frog.
It is a kiwi.

Lauren Ellis (5)
The Meads Primary School, East Grinstead

A Kiwi

As furry as a carpet
As slippery as a fish
As slimy as a frog
As green as a bush
As sweet as a marshmallow
What is it?

Molly Sutton (5)
The Meads Primary School, East Grinstead

Pomegranate

It is as pink as a flower
It is as hard as a rock
It is as juicy as orange juice
It has a spiky crown.

Ciara Fitzsimons (5)
The Meads Primary School, East Grinstead

A Kiwi

As juicy as apple juice
As green as peas
As soft as a cat
As soft as sugar cherry sweets.

Finley Smith (5)
The Meads Primary School, East Grinstead

A Pomegranate

As round as a ball.
As sweet as Haribo.
As red as a postbox.
It has seeds in it.
Can you guess what it is?

Charlie Snashfold (5)
The Meads Primary School, East Grinstead

A Kiwi

As green as a bush.
As sour as lemonade.
As furry as a hamster.
As squishy as jelly.
What is it?

Sophie Bowes (5)
The Meads Primary School, East Grinstead

Grapes

It is as sweet as apple juice
It is juicy like cucumber
They can be red or green
There could be some seeds inside
What is it?

Nicole Painter (5)
The Meads Primary School, East Grinstead

Who Am I?

I have a wife called Victoria.
I am a famous football player.
I am as skinny as Miss Crouch.
I have a cool smile.
I have a white football kit.
I have short hair.
I am as cool as Peter Crouch.
I score a lot of goals.

Ron Molloy (6)
Viking Primary School, Northolt

What Am I?

I am fluffy
I am soft
I am black
I am white.

Erin Howe (7)
Viking Primary School, Northolt

What Am I?

I am bigger than a pig.
I am white and I have huge black spots.
I can shake my ears.
I have milk.
I live on a farm.
I like to eat grass.
What am I?

Yasmin Reza (7)
Viking Primary School, Northolt

What Am I?

I am fluffy and brown
I am crazy
I love bananas
I have a long tail
I jump as high as King Kong
I live in the jungle
What am I?

Suheyb Abdullahi (6)
Viking Primary School, Northolt

What Am I?

I am fluffy like a puppy.
I have an orange beak for food to pick.
I swim like a fish.
I slide in a swish.
I am very, very cute.
I have a black and white suit.
I love snow and I live in an igloo.
I am a penguin.

Inara Paindazadah (6)
Viking Primary School, Northolt

Who Am I?

I am an ugly and frightening animal
With a long tail that can climb trees
Who am I?
I am a monkey.

Muhsin (6)
Viking Primary School, Northolt

What Am I?

I eat people
I chase people
I am yellow
What am I?

Dilumi Warnakulasuriya (6)
Viking Primary School, Northolt

Who Am I?

I have a long nose.
I have two teeth.
I have a gigantic face.
I have a grey face.
I have a grey body.
I am like a kangaroo.
I have a long trunk.
I am an elephant.

Genevieve Lanyero-Banya (6)
Viking Primary School, Northolt

What Am I?

I am brown on the outside
and on the inside I am beautiful, green and juicy.
I have beautiful black seeds.
What am I?
I am a kiwi.

Aurella Brzezowska (7)
Viking Primary School, Northolt

What Am I?

I am the king of Africa.
I am yellow like a tiger.
I can eat people.
I am very dangerous like a shark.
I can see in the dark.
I can eat animals.
What am I?
A lion.

Arthur Simcenco (6)
Viking Primary School, Northolt

What Am I?

I am a king.
I can roar like a tiger.
I have gigantic long claws.
I can run as fast as a sports car.
What am I?

Isaiah Willie (7)
Viking Primary School, Northolt

What Am I?

I have four legs
I have one tail
I have fluffy hair
People love me
I am different colours
I love to eat rats and mice
What am I?

Faiz Zahid (6)
Viking Primary School, Northolt

Who Am I?

I wear a yellow dress like the golden sun.
I am gorgeous like a rose.
My hair is as brown as crispy leaves.
I have round yellow earrings.
I wear long yellow gloves like a rope.
I have a yellow hairband that looks like a circle.
I wear yellow high heels.
Who am I?
Belle.

Laila Younis (6)
Viking Primary School, Northolt

What Am I?

I am cute and small
about an inch tall.
I run in a wheel
eat sunflower seeds and corn
just a small meal.
I live in a cage and sleep all day.
In the night I come out to play.
What am I?

Kai Brooks (6)
Viking Primary School, Northolt

Animal Fun

It has eight massive legs
It glows in the dark
It's fast
It has a powerful sting
It is wild
It spits venom
It can pounce
It can eat lizards
And it can kill humans

It is a wandering spider.

Hugh Werry (6)
Wrestlingworth Lower School, Wrestlingworth

What Is It?

It has four legs
It can run quickly
It can jump
It eats daisies
It eats carrots
It has silver fur

It is a rabbit.

Megan Butt (6)
Wrestlingworth Lower School, Wrestlingworth

The Riddle Of A Lizard

It has four legs
It has a sticky tongue
It has a long tail
It has spikes
It eats crickets and mealworms
It has sharp claws
It is a lizard.

James Ellis-Crease (6)
Wrestlingworth Lower School, Wrestlingworth

What Is It?

It has no legs
It slithers and slides
It has silver scales
It lives in long grass
It eats rats and mice
It has red eyes
It can see very well

It is a snake.

Colin Seward (6)
Wrestlingworth Lower School, Wrestlingworth

Young Writers Information

We hope you have enjoyed reading this book - and that you will continue to enjoy it in the coming years.
If you like reading and writing poetry drop us a line, or give us a call, and we'll send you a free information pack.
Alternatively if you would like to order further copies of this book or any of our other titles, then please give us a call or log onto our website at www.youngwriters.co.uk.

Young Writers Information
Remus House
Coltsfoot Drive
Peterborough
PE2 9BF
(01733) 890066